STRUGGLE FOR SURVIVAL

Water

William B. Rice

Consultants

Timothy Rasinski, Ph.D.
Kent State University

Lori Oczkus, M.A.
Literacy Consultant

Christopher Nyerges
Author and Educator;
Cofounder of School of Self-Reliance

Publishing Credits

Rachelle Cracchiolo, M.S.Ed., *Publisher*
Conni Medina, M.A.Ed., *Managing Editor*
Dona Herweck Rice, *Series Developer*
Emily R. Smith, M.A.Ed., *Content Director*
Stephanie Bernard and Seth Rogers, *Editors*
Robin Erickson, *Multimedia Designer*

The TIME logo is a registered trademark of TIME Inc. Used under license.

Image Credits: p.18 Phil Degginger/Science Source; pp.33–35
Illustrations by Kevin Pham; pp.36–37 Shaiith/Dreamstime.com; All
other images from iStock and/or Shutterstock.

Notes: Care and caution should always be practiced when using tools
and methods for survival. The answers to the mathematics problems
posed throughout the book are provided on page 48.

Library of Congress Cataloging-in-Publication Data

Names: Rice, William B. (William Benjamin), 1961- author.
Title: Struggle for survival. Water / William B. Rice.
Other titles: Water
Description: Huntington Beach, CA : Teacher Created Materials, [2016] |
  Audience: Grades 4 to 6. | Includes bibliographical references and
index.
Identifiers: LCCN 2016016965 (print) | LCCN 2016017502 (ebook) | ISBN
  9781493836031 (pbk.) | ISBN 9781480757073 (eBook)
Subjects: LCSH: Survival--Juvenile literature.
Classification: LCC GF86 .R5257 2016 (print) | LCC GF86 (ebook) | DDC
  613.6/9--dc23
LC record available at https://lccn.loc.gov/2016016965

Teacher Created Materials
5301 Oceanus Drive
Huntington Beach, CA 92649-1030
http://www.tcmpub.com

ISBN 978-1-4938-3603-1
© 2017 Teacher Created Materials, Inc.
Printed in China

Table of Contents

What Do I Do Now?

You weren't expecting it. You didn't see it coming, and it caught you completely by surprise. Life has taken a sudden, drastic turn, and a new reality has taken its place. Unfortunately, in this reality, your very survival is at stake.

You're hungry, thirsty, tired, cold, and suddenly alone. All the resources that were easily accessible to you just a short time ago have suddenly disappeared. All the government systems and agencies that you count on regularly are unavailable. You can't be certain what's really going on because your ability to communicate with others is limited. Cell phones? Not now. There's no water coming from your faucet. There's no power in your home, either, so refrigeration is not an option. What about your food? What if your cupboards are empty and there's nothing available to purchase at the stores? You *must* eat to survive, and you *must* have water. In fact, water is more important than almost anything else. But where will you get these precious things that your well-being—and your very life—depend on? What will you do, and more importantly, how will you survive?

Or *will* you?

THINK LINK

- What types of things could happen to create a **doomsday scenario**?

- What basic skills do you think are necessary to help you survive?

- Describe any **survival skills** you already have.

What *Is* Survival?

Survival has become a popular topic in recent years. There are television shows that depict survival situations. And there are reality game shows in which survival is part of the game. You can even learn about survival in books, Internet videos, blogs, websites, and magazines.

But what is survival exactly? It depends on whom you ask. You are likely to find many different answers.

At its root, *survival* means to keep living. No one lives forever. But most people want to live long, enjoyable lives. Much of modern life has been dedicated to extending the human life span. At the same time, people have become dependent on **industry** to support survival. And we have created lifestyles that may separate us from more traditional, and perhaps even natural, ways to survive. Most people in modern cultures lack the skills that humans have depended on to survive and thrive for thousands of years.

I Didn't Expect That!

What could possibly happen to create a doomsday scenario? The truth is, such a scenario is highly unlikely. The following types of events that require survival skills are more likely to happen:

- ◎ an accident in the wilderness far from help (a rock slide, a tumble down a steep slope, etc.)

- ◎ a natural disaster, such as an earthquake, a tornado, or a hurricane

- ◎ getting lost in the wilderness

- ◎ an automobile accident or breakdown in the middle of nowhere

Methods and Tools

Most of us depend on our modern way of life to survive. Healthy, clean, hot and cold water are available in our houses at the turn of a knob. We have heaters to keep us warm. Air conditioners keep us cool. We can buy clothes easily in stores. Food is available in restaurants and stores all around us. So, what can we use to help us learn to survive in emergency situations?

Today, learning to survive involves the use of methods and tools. What methods and tools are needed? Well, some methods may involve having different survival **strategies** at your fingertips. The strategies can be used in any number of unusual situations. For example, one strategy may be ways to find clean water. Another may be methods to keep your body warm. The tools are devices people can use as part of each strategy to survive. They may be things we already have, such as knives, blankets, or other things made in factories. They may also be **primitive**, or handmade from **repurposed** or natural materials. One survival strategy may be knowing how to make these things!

Changes to a person's current way of life may have **dire** consequences. That is especially true if the person doesn't have the basic knowledge needed to survive.

You Need Every Drop

Experts agree that you need about two quarts (64 ounces) of drinking water each day. In extreme weather or if you exercise a lot, you need about a gallon (128 ounces) a day. Under normal conditions, how much water would a family of four need to survive one week, in quarts, ounces, and gallons?

Everyday Carry

To be prepared for emergency situations, some people carry small basic tools with them all the time. These tools might include a whistle or a multi-tool pocket knife. These are called everyday carry, or EDC. Equally smart is learning to make tools out of objects found in nature.

The Most Important Things to Remember

There is a lot to learn about survival, and it can feel overwhelming. Most experts agree, though, that there are a few key principles to remember. These key principles will help increase your chances of survival.

Preparation

The longtime scouting motto is "Be Prepared," and there's a good reason for that. It is important to be aware of your location and home environment. When you travel, it is important to be aware of your destination's environment, too.

Another aspect of **preparation** involves being properly skilled. It is important to prepare yourself in case of emergency situations. Do you know how to start a campfire and keep it going? Do you know how to make a shelter? Do you know where and how to find water and food? And if you do have these skills, do you also have the proper equipment and supplies available?

Deep Breaths

If you find yourself becoming overwhelmed, sit down and breathe. Taking long, deep breaths calms the body and mind and gives you time to return to more relaxed levels.

Fight or Flight?

Maybe you do begin to panic. You think dire thoughts, your heart rate increases, you feel short of breath, and your body starts to shake. You are primed to fight—or ready to run. This is called the *fight or flight response*. It is a natural response that has helped humans and other animals survive challenging situations.

Composure

In a survival scenario, nothing matters more than **composure**. Survival expert Cody Lundin outlines a five-point plan to keep anyone in the right frame of mind. He calls it *STOPA*: **S**top, **T**hink, **O**bserve, **P**lan, and **A**ct. Following the five steps will help you maintain your composure.

In emergencies, we can become fearful, but panicking makes situations worse. Be aware of your emotions, and try your best to manage your responses. Especially in an emergency, this will enhance your chances for survival.

Strategy

It's important to come up with a plan to help keep you focused. Develop a strategy. You can do this by observing and assessing your environment. Then, think about your **priorities**. What things do you need to consider first? The following are key priorities to think about:

- secure personal safety
- maintain body temperature
- maintain body **hydration**

Putting these three things first, preferably in this order, will go a long way toward your survival. Consider these, and then decide on a response to your situation.

In the Zone

Normal average body temperature is 98.6°Fahrenheit (37°Celsius). It is normal for a person's temperature to go up or down from that number by about 1.1°F (0.6°C). What is the normal range of body temperature in both Fahrenheit and Celsius?

Action

You've kept your cool, followed priorities, and made a plan. Now, it's time to act on your decisions and commit to them. But stay aware, and keep assessing. Continually assess your environment, circumstances, and personal conditions. How is your plan working? Are you getting the desired results? Remember to **adapt** as needed. This will increase your chances of survival.

If your plan includes moving from one place to another, you might discover a new option. Be ready to take advantage of any new opportunities and circumstances. Maybe you planned to build a shelter, but in looking for materials, you find an existing shelter. Maybe you find an unexpected water source. Or perhaps you come upon animals or people that may be dangerous. In any case, be smart and be patient with yourself and your decisions.

THINK LINK

In a survival scenario, it's important to think and get oriented in terms of time and location. Ask yourself the following questions.

- ◎ **Time:** What time of day and what time of year is it? How much daylight do I have left? About how long will darkness last? Is air temperature going to get hotter or colder?

- ◎ **Location:** From which direction did I come? Which direction is uphill? Which direction is downhill? How far am I from the nearest community? Where is the nearest emergency station (firehouse, police station, etc.)?

Can You Survive?

The most important tool in a survival scenario is your brain. You've got to think about and assess your current conditions. After a little time passes, think again. Conditions change, and you should always adapt your plans to the conditions.

Do you have what it takes to survive? Can you successfully assess your situation? Take this quiz to find out!

1. You are lost in the wilderness. You . . .

   a. panic.

   b. climb a tree.

   c. hunt for food.

   d. think about the resources you have and how to use them.

2. Your car has broken down in the middle of the desert. You . . .

   a. go to sleep until someone finds you.

   b. drink all your water.

   c. start walking because you're bound to run into help.

   d. think about the conditions you are in and make a plan to survive them until you can change them.

3. You've just survived a terrible tornado. Everything around you is flattened. You . . .

    a. just sit and cry because, after all, you're in a tough situation.

    b. randomly start poking in the wreckage.

    c. hide because another tornado may be on its way.

    d. look around, gather resources, and make a plan for survival.

If you answered *d* to every question, you're on the right track! Always use your brain to assess . . .

- yourself
- the situation
- the environment
- your tools and equipment

Remember: You don't have to guess! You can be your best and pass any test if you simply assess!

Water Is Life and Death

"When the well's dry, we know the worth of water."
—**Benjamin Franklin**

You know and understand now the basic keys to survival. But none of that knowledge means much of anything without water. Water is essential for life. For people, it is even more important than food. This is because water is a big portion of our blood and is in all our cells. We can't live without it.

The specific amount of water each person needs depends on his or her size and age. It also depends on the outside temperature and the body's activity. For example, the more you sweat, the more water you need to **replenish** what is lost.

People lose water in different ways. It is lost mainly through urination, perspiration, and respiration. These are part of the way the human body works to keep us healthy, so there is no way to avoid them. But perspiration and respiration can be limited to help maintain hydration.

Amazing Camels

Some camels can survive about 180 days without drinking water. The longest humans can survive without water is about 7 days. How many times longer can camels survive without water than humans?

17

Changing Attitudes

The first peoples camped or lived near steady and reliable water sources. To stay hydrated and healthy, civilizations were developed near these bodies of water.

Today, in many parts of the world, people tend to take water for granted. We can get water so easily that there isn't much reason to think about it. Unfortunately, easy access to water can make us treat it without care. We throw trash and debris into oceans, lakes, rivers, and streams.

Early people did not treat water so carelessly. They had great respect for water. They knew how vital it was for life. It seems the more civilized we became as societies, the more poorly we treated our water supplies. Things like water filters and bottled water made it easier for us to mistreat natural sources.

Beware Bacteria!

Bacteria in **tainted** water may make a person sick. At best, water bacteria can cause diarrhea, vomiting, and stomach cramps. At worst, bacteria can eat away at the body and cause the thirsty person to become gravely ill and eventually die. So, be careful before you start drinking any untreated water!

There is bacteria in this water.

When Water Is Needed

We are used to having drinking water available. But in a survival scenario, water may not be easy to get. It may have to be found. And if that's the case, you must keep a few things in mind:

- **Quality:** Is the available water polluted or **unpotable**?

- **Access:** Is the available water in a dangerous or difficult-to-access location?

- **Equipment:** Do you have what you need to boil the water for safe drinking?

Safety First!

If you don't know with absolute certainty that water is safe to drink, boil it or treat it first . . . *always!* See pages 26–27 for more information about how to treat water.

Cities are responsible for protecting their water sources.

Conserving Bodily Fluids

In an emergency, you need to conserve the water that is already in your body. But how do you restrict water loss?

During the day, get into the shade and stay there. It also helps to minimize physical activity when it is hot. If you must be active, do it in the evening when the sun has gone down but it is not fully dark yet. You can also be more active in the early morning when there is enough light to see but the sun has not fully risen. And be sure to perform any activities at steady, even paces to minimize overexertion and perspiration.

Digestion uses a large amount of water in the body. Remember, you can live much longer without food than without water. So, unless you absolutely need to, do not eat.

Even if you're hot, keep your clothes on and cover your head as well. You will lose more moisture if your skin is directly exposed to the air. Try to stay out of the wind as much as possible, since wind also increases water loss.

If you have an ample water supply, make sure you drink lots of clean water. Don't take even a small chance of dehydrating yourself.

The Pinch Test

To test a person for dehydration, pinch the skin on the back of his or her hand. If the skin snaps back quickly, then the person is likely fine. If the skin returns to its normal shape slowly, the person may be dehydrated.

From an Expert

Survivalist Dave Arama offers this advice for conserving water and energy in our bodies:

- If you don't have to stand, sit.
- If you don't have to sit, lie down.
- Minimize talking, which takes effort and increases respiration.
- Breathe through your nose, since mouth breathing releases more water.

Finding Water

Remember the survival priorities mentioned earlier? If you do, you know what you need to do first. You need to secure your safety and develop a plan to address **exposure**. Assuming you have done those things, you can and should address your body's need for a steady supply of water. You should start to think about and plan how to find water.

The key to finding water is not necessarily the method to collect it. Instead, the key is understanding water itself and knowing where to find it. In other words, it's not *how* to get it so much as *where* to get it.

60%

Tall Drink of Water

Adults are made up of about 60% water. The average adult human body has a volume of 66.4L. So, how much of that overall volume is water?

Movies often show heroes in dire straits, using clever methods to obtain water. But most movies' goals are to create drama and suspense, not to depict reality. Remember that these movies are not instructional videos. Do not count on the film industry to provide practical guidelines for survival. The methods may look cool, but if you try to follow them to protect your life, you're likely to wind up very thirsty—or worse.

So, how do *you*—a real person in the real world—find water?

Heat Exhaustion

Prolonged exposure to heat can result in heat exhaustion—or worse, heatstroke. Signs of heat exhaustion include heavy sweating, dizziness, weak and rapid pulse, feeling faint, nausea, headache, and more. Heatstroke may include all these plus fainting, a high fever, and hot, dry skin because the person has stopped sweating from loss of water.

First things first. Look around you to check out water availability in obvious sources such as creeks, streams, and lakes. You can also look for snow, ice, or slush, which are merely frozen water. While looking around, you'll quickly be able to answer, "Yes, I have a water supply" or "No, there's no water in sight."

Yes, I Have a Water Supply

If your answer is *yes*, then you are in relatively good shape. You just need to make sure that the water is clean enough to drink. You should assume that all water is **contaminated**. You'll need to treat any and all water before you drink it, unless you are completely certain the water is safe. (Read about treating water on pages 26–27.)

If snow, ice, and slush are available, they can be melted to drink, but you'll need a container to store the water. Of course, just as with any water, be sure to decontaminate it by boiling or treating it so it's safe.

Signs of Dehydration

Dehydration is a serious issue. It is important to know the symptoms. Symptoms of dehydration include headaches, nausea, poor judgment, depression, and dark yellow urine. If a person is not urinating at all, then he or she is likely dehydrated.

No, There's No Water in Sight

If your answer is *no*, you will need to find water in a situation where it is not obvious. There are many ways to do this, and some will surprise you. Keep reading to find out how to do this!

Treating Water

Having safe water to drink is extremely vital. So, knowing how to treat water is an essential skill to learn. Here are three ways to treat water so that it is safe for drinking.

Boiling

This is the easiest method to decontaminate water. Boil the water for 10 minutes. In high elevations (above 5,000 feet or 1,524 meters), boil it an additional minute for each 1,000 feet (304.8 meters) of elevation above sea level. Keep the pot covered to avoid as much evaporation as possible. Be sure to let the water cool before drinking it.

How Long?

Determine how long you will boil water to purify it at 5,000 feet. How long at 7,000 feet? How long at 10,000 feet?

Bleaching

Using an eyedropper, add 16 drops of chlorine bleach to each gallon (3.8 liters) of water. Use liquid chlorine bleach that is 5% to 6% sodium hypochlorite with no additives or preservatives. Mix and let stand for 30 minutes. The water should smell slightly of bleach. If it doesn't, add 16 more drops and let it stand for 15 minutes. If it still doesn't smell of bleach, the water is too contaminated to drink.

Distilling

This method is a lot harder and less successful than the other two, but it works with the right equipment. With this method, you can also rid saltwater of salt to make it drinkable. Put the water in a large pot. Tie a cup to the pot handle, with the opening of the cup placed toward the pot lid. Place the lid on the pot. The cup should not touch the water. Boil the water for 20 minutes. Evaporating water that is clean and distilled will hit the lid and condense into the cup. There won't be much of it, but it is safe to drink.

Observe the Environment

One crucial way to find water is to study the **topography**. There is water in most soils; however, finding enough water to drink is the challenge. Sometimes, finding water can be as easy as walking. Walking downhill might lead you to a water source. Water flows downhill and collects in valley bottoms. Even the water flowing underground flows downhill. Seeps and springs will probably be located a little farther up than the valley bottom, but they can also be found at many locations along the valley—so pay close attention. Creeks and streams may flow back underground before running along the surface. There may also be water in what appears to be dry riverbeds or creek beds, especially at their bends, but you may need to dig down to find it.

Water may be in **catchments** under rocks as well. And pay special attention to the color and location of vegetation. Fertile and healthy vegetation must have a water source to grow, so look around and dig.

In the Mountains

Water is probably easier to find in mountains than in deserts. Snow and ice are typically more common in mountains. Look on north-facing slopes and in hollows. Look for deep **fissures** and valleys in mountainsides where water may have accumulated.

Follow Animal Trails

Animals aren't just fun to watch—they can also help you find water. Birds, insects, and small animals that live in an area know where the water is. They couldn't live there if they didn't. Follow them, and you may find water.

In the Desert

Prickly pear cactus is a plant found in many deserts. To get the water from the plant, scrape the needles from the young prickly pear pads, cut the pads into pieces, and chew them. You don't really extract the water, but you "eat" the water instead.

prickly pear cactus

Collect Dew and Rain

In many places, there is condensation in the form of dew in the early morning hours. Dew can be collected from the leaves of some plants, or it can be gathered on a tarp or sheet of plastic. Ideally, the dew can be collected in a container to store and use over time.

Know What You've Got

You have a 55-gallon rain barrel that is 60% full. With the amount of water currently in it, how many gallons of water are available to you in an emergency situation?

Seawater

It shouldn't be a problem to get safe water from the ocean, right? Wrong. Trying to consume salty seawater can be challenging or even impossible. If it rains, take advantage of the great opportunity. Catching rainwater will help you make salt water safer to drink. Rainwater can be mixed with seawater to increase the supply. To be safe, make sure you mix in at least half rainwater. In a survival situation, drinking a mixture of sea water and rainwater is all right.

Rain can be a saving grace in a survival situation. You can drink rain as it falls, or you can collect it in a container. Collecting rainwater is a great way to ensure you have a water supply to last you. If you don't have a container, you can make one using a sheet of plastic. You can dig a hole and line it with the plastic to catch rainwater. Shells, bark, and other natural materials, if shaped in the right way, may also be able to catch and hold rainwater. The more containers you have, the better.

Make a Vegetation Still or a Solar Still

What if you have done some searching and some digging and have still not found any water? Well, you still have options. The following two water-collection ideas are a little more involved but have been shown to work. One option is a vegetation still, and the other is a solar still. For these, you need a couple of key items.

For the vegetation still, you need a large, clear plastic bag and some cord. Plants release water through their leaves back into the atmosphere in a process called **transpiration**. To capture the water, tie a plastic bag around the leafy end of a tree branch or bush. The more leaves, the better. Willow or oak trees are probably best, but others work also. Tie the cord tightly around the opening of the bag so no air can escape. Wait for a while, but check the bag occasionally to make sure the cord is tight enough and the still is working properly. After a while, water released from the leaves will start collecting in the bag. When there is enough to drink, carefully remove the bag from the plant so that you don't spill the water or tear the bag.

Success!

Survival expert Christopher Nyerges has performed nearly 100 experiments on the two stills. He has found that vegetation stills produce 25% to 50% more water than solar stills.

vegetation still

Do the Math

If a solar still produces 1 liter of water over a day, about how much more water might you expect from a vegetation still of the same capacity over 7 days if it produces 25% more water? How about 50% more water?

To make a solar still, you need a large sheet of plastic and a wide-mouth container. You will be collecting water that evaporates from the ground. Find a location where you suspect the soil underground may be moist. Dig a hole about three feet (one meter) wide and three feet (one meter) deep. Place the container in the middle of the hole and surround it with plant material, such as grass or cactus. Place the plastic sheet over the hole, and pull the edges so it is suspended over the hole. Place rocks on the edges of the plastic to hold it in place and seal the hole. Place a small stone in the middle of the plastic, directly over the container. This should cause the middle of the sheet to drop below the level of the edges.

During the day, the sun will cause water to evaporate from the soil and plant material. Water will collect on the underside of the plastic, flow downhill, and drip into the container. Periodically check on the still to see how it is working and whether adjustments are needed.

Natural Disaster

In natural disasters like earthquakes, your water supply may be cut off. However, your house may still have plenty of water. Water heaters can hold about 189 liters (50 gallons). Water can even be found in pipes or in toilet tanks. And, of course, swimming pools hold several thousand liters of water. But be careful! Swimming pools usually contain chlorine. This water may need to be decontaminated.

Believe It or Not

It may sound gross, but you can urinate into the hole for a solar still. The water in urine will evaporate just like other water. And distilled (evaporated) water is quite pure and safe to drink.

In Consideration of Food

In survival situations, the first thing that many people think about is having enough to eat. This makes sense for many reasons. We all need food to live. Food gives the body fuel, structure, and **nutrients**. For many of us, our daily schedule revolves around meals. But in a survival situation, food is not always a priority. Most of us can live adequately without food for about three weeks. Looking for, preparing, and processing food can use up important time and energy. That time and energy might be better spent building a shelter or finding water.

Emotional Boost

Sometimes in normal life, people turn to food for comfort. That's not always a healthy choice. But in a survival situation, food may also provide emotional comfort and a psychological boost. It is important to remember, though, that survival depends more on water than food.

Side Effects of Fasting

While we can go quite long without food, it's not an easy thing to endure. There are hunger pangs, and you might notice sluggishness, fatigue, or loss of energy. The best thing to do is be aware of what you are experiencing, get some rest, and conserve your energy.

Also, after two or three days of **fasting**, the body's metabolism begins to change. After two weeks, the body uses the fuel and nutrients already stored in it much more efficiently.

Finally, digestion requires a lot of water. So, if you have a very limited water supply, it's probably not a good idea to eat. Only eat if you have a reliable and stable supply of water on hand.

WARNING

Many wild plants are poisonous. Never eat any wild foods unless you know for sure that they are safe.

Learn Your Local Foods

When it comes to food, nothing is more important than planning and preparing. If you're in a city or a town during a survival situation, finding food is probably less difficult. But what do you do if you are in the middle of nowhere, surrounded only by nature and wilderness?

Getting food from the natural environment is not an easy task. When it comes to **foraging**, hunting, and trapping, there are no shortcuts. This is where planning and preparing come in. To obtain food, you must know what sorts of plants and animals are available. It is important to study and develop skills if you want to have food in a survival situation. For instance, it can be helpful to know which plants are safe to eat. Developing these skills takes time and effort! You can read books to help you, or you can spend time in nature exploring with experts.

Any time and effort spent learning about local foods will also build confidence and awareness. It is rewarding and provides more than a little peace of mind. You'll know what to look for and what to do with it once you find it!

Acorns

Acorns are the fruit of oak trees, and oak trees are found all over the world. To eat an acorn, first crack the shell. Remove the seed, or meat, from the shell. Then **leach** the seed. You do this by repeatedly boiling the meat in water for one to three hours to remove the bitter taste. You will need to change the water several times while doing this.

Prickly Pear Cactus

You already know that a good source of water in the desert is the prickly pear cactus. The pads can also be eaten raw or cooked. Prickly pears produce fruit that can be eaten as well, and the seeds inside them can be ground and eaten.

Natural Disasters

Unfortunately, different kinds of natural disasters, including earthquakes, tornadoes, and hurricanes, happen regularly in various places. Many people may lose their lives in these events, and even more people may be left without the resources they need for survival. Such resources include water, food, candles, and blankets, among other things. What can people do to get the food they need in these disruptive situations?

Insects . . . Yum?

Insects are a healthy and nutritious source of nutrition. Many contain as much protein per pound as meat or fish. It is recommended that adult men should take in about 60 grams of protein each day. A 3.5-ounce serving of raw grasshoppers contains about 15 grams of protein. How many ounces of grasshoppers would an adult man need to eat to take in the recommended 60 grams of protein in one day?

The best thing to do is to be ready. We know that these events will happen again sometime. We don't know exactly when or how things will turn out, but we do know they are coming, so it's important to plan and prepare. One way to plan ahead for such disasters is by stocking up on **nonperishable** food items. Store dry foods, canned foods, and dried foods. Dry foods include nuts, seeds, and grains. Canned foods include canned corn, peas, and green beans. And dried foods are things such as dried fruit, beans, rice, or jerkies. Foods prepared in these ways can be stored for long periods of time and remain **edible**. Be sure to store nutritious foods you like to eat.

Be Prepared and Keep Your Cool

Even in a dire situation, there's always hope as long as you remain calm and use your brain. And most importantly, things are guaranteed to be even better if you stay thoughtful and prepared. That doesn't mean you always have to worry about bad things happening and try to prepare for every possibility. That's impossible, and more than that, worry takes the joy out of life. When we look at things realistically, we realize that most days, everything is fine. Survival isn't typically an issue, but challenges do arise. One day, you may need to rely on your skills, preparation, and brainpower to get through an emergency. If so, don't panic! You are up to the task. In fact, you can help others by staying calm, keeping cool, and remembering your survival priorities:

- secure personal safety

- maintain body temperature

- maintain body hydration

You *know* what to do. Now, get out there and do more than just survive—*live*!

Those Amazing, Adaptable Human Beings!

Many factors have helped the human species survive for more than 200,000 years. One of the most important is the fascinating and **analytic** human brain. Other factors include adaptable bodies and the ability to cooperate with one another. You have these same capabilities. So use them to their fullest!

Glossary

adapt—to change to fit a new or specific situation or circumstance

analytic—thinking about something by focusing on its parts

catchments—things that catch water

composure—calmness of mind

contaminated—infected, soiled, or tainted

digestion—the process of breaking down food inside the body to get its nourishment

dire—horrible; disastrous

doomsday scenario—a situation that marks the end of the world as it has been known

edible—safe to be eaten

exposure—the act of being open to extreme weather conditions for a dangerous amount of time; unprotected

fasting—not eating for periods of time

fissures—small openings or cracks

foraging—the act of looking for and gathering food from the wild

hydration—the act of having a sufficient supply of fluids, especially water

industry—business and manufacturing

leach—to pass a liquid through something to carry away unwanted and dissolvable parts

nonperishable—unlikely to spoil or decay

nutrients—things that provide the substances necessary for a body's health and growth

preparation—the action or process of making yourself ready in advance

primitive—quite basic; made by a self-taught artisan

priorities—things that deserve attention before others

replenish—to fill up again

repurposed—recycled; remade from existing materials

strategies—plans

survival skills—abilities to provide for the basic needs of life

tainted—contaminated; spoiled

topography—the shapes, heights, and depths of the land

transpiration—the process by which plants give off water vapor

unpotable—unsuitable for drinking

Index

Check It Out!

Books

George, Jean Craighead. 2004. *My Side of the Mountain*. Puffin Books.

Nyerges, Christopher. 2014. *How to Survive Anywhere: A Guide for Urban, Suburban, Rural, and Wilderness Environments*. Stackpole Books.

O'Dell, Scott. 2010. *Island of the Blue Dolphins*. HMH Books for Young Readers.

Olsen, Larry Dean. 1990. *Outdoor Survival Skills*. Chicago Review Press.

Paulsen, Gary. 2006. *Hatchet*. Simon & Schuster Books for Young Readers.

Rice, William B. 2013. *Survival! Desert*. Teacher Created Materials.

_____. 2013. *Survival! Jungle*. Teacher Created Materials.

_____. 2013. *Survival! Ocean*. Teacher Created Materials.

Society of Primitive Technology. 2014. *Bulletin of Primitive Technology*. Rexburg, ID: Society of Primitive Technology.

Websites

Lundin, Cody. *Aboriginal Living Skills School*. http://www.codylundin.com/.

Noble, Christian. *Master Woodsman*. http://masterwoodsman.com/.

Nyerges, Christopher. *School of Self-Reliance*. http://www.christophernyerges.com/.

Magazines

Richie, Charlie (ed.). *The Backwoodsman*. Backwoodsman Magazine.

Try It!

You and your friend are stranded on a deserted island. There are no people around, no civilization, and no way to get off the island. You are going to be there until search parties find you. Using the information that you have read in this book, come up with a plan to face this situation.

- ◎ Describe in images or words the first thing you would do.

- ◎ If there was no natural source of water, what method (or methods) of collecting water would you use?

- ◎ Once you have a method for collecting water, where would you store the extra water you collect?

- ◎ After your water is planned for, describe your next concern.

- ◎ If you have to wait for more than a month, how might your plan change?

About the Author

William B. Rice is a native Californian who enjoys the fundamental skills involved in survival as well as the simple and traditional ways of life. Bill is a geologist who works for the state of California to protect water quality. He is passionate about the well-being of planet Earth. Bill has authored many books for children on science topics, especially those concerned with the environment and protecting it. He enjoys spending time outdoors and is an avid camper, hiker, and naturalist. He lives in the Inland Empire with his wife and sons.

Answers

page 8—56 quarts,1,792 ounces, 14 gallons
page 12—97.5°F–99.7°F (36.4°C–37.6°C)
page 16—25.7 (about 26) times longer than humans
page 22—39.84L
page 26—10 min. at 5,000 ft., 12 min. at 7,000 ft., 15 min. at 10,000 ft.
page 30—33 gallons
page 33—8.75 L (25% more) or 10.5 L (50% more)
page 40—14 ounces of grasshoppers